I0814569

SCIENTIFIC AMERICAN EDUCATIONAL PUBLISHING

CHEMISTRY MAGIC

10 FUN CHEMISTRY EXPERIMENTS

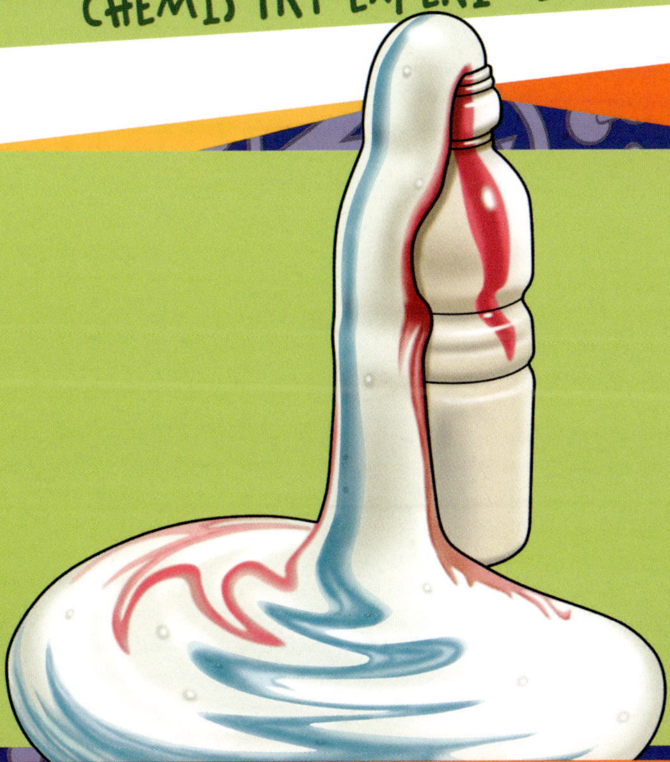

BRING SCIENCE HOME

Published in 2023 by The Rosen Publishing Group, Inc.
2544 Clinton St, Buffalo, NY 14224

First Edition

Editor: Kristen Nelson
Designer: Rachel Rising

Activity on p. 5 by Science Buddies/Svenja Lohner (September 5, 2019); p. 11 by Science Buddie/ Ben Finio (August 1, 2019); p. 15 by Science Buddies/Svenja Lohner (November 15, 2018); p. 19 by Science Buddies/Megan Arnett (July 19, 2018); 23 by Science Buddies/Megan Arnett (May 24, 2018); p. 29 by Science Buddies/Svenja Lohner (May 10, 2018); p. 35 by Science Buddies/Megan Arnett (March 1, 2018); p. 43 by Science Buddies/Ben Finio (February 8, 2018); p. 49 by Science Buddies/Sabine De Brabandere (January 25, 2018); p. 55 by Science Buddies/Svenja Lohner (December 14, 2017).

Photo Credits: pp. 4, 8, 13, 14, 17, 18, 26, 29, 33, 39, 45, 46, 49, 52, 55, 58, 59 cve iv/Shutterstock.com; pp. 5, 11, 15, 19, 23, 29, 35, 43, 49, 55 Anna Frajtova/Shutterstock.com.

All illustrations by Continuum Content Solutions

Cataloging-in-Publication Data
Names: Scientific American, inc.
Title: Chemistry magic / edited by the Editors of Scientific American.
Description: Buffalo, New York : Scientific American Educational Publishing, 2023. | Series: Bring science home | Includes glossary and index.
Identifiers: ISBN 9781684169849 (pbk.) | ISBN 9781684169856 (library bound) | ISBN 9781684169863 (ebook)
Subjects: LCSH: Chemistry--Experiments--Juvenile literature. | Science projects--Juvenile literature.
Classification: LCC QD43.C446 2023 | DDC 540.78--dc23

Manufactured in the United States of America

Some of the images in this book illustrate individuals who are models. The depictions do not imply actual situations or events.

CPSIA Compliance Information: Batch #SACS23. For further information contact Rosen Publishing at 1-800-237-9932.

CONTENTS

INTRODUCTION

Do you ever wonder if your shampoo is working well? Or how laundry detergent cleans stains off your clothing? It's chemistry! The results of the following experiments might seem like magic, but everything that happens—from the soapiest suds you've ever seen to batteries made using pennies and washers—is pure science.

Projects marked with include a section called Science Fair Project ideas. These ideas can help you develop your own original science fair project. Science fair judges tend to reward creative thought and imagination, and it helps if you are really interested in your project. You will also need to follow the scientific method. See page 61 for more information about that.

Make a Candle Flame Jump

ILLUMINATING SCIENCE: LEARN WHAT KEEPS A CANDLE BURNING—AND HOW YOU CAN LIGHT A CANDLE ALMOST OUT OF THIN AIR.

There are many occasions to light candles. Have you ever looked closely at the flame? Which part of the candle is actually burning? Can you tell? Is it the wick, the solid wax, the liquid wax, or something else? In this activity, you will light some candles to find out—no special occasion required!

PROJECT TIME

20–30 minutes

KEY CONCEPTS

Chemistry
Chemical reactions
States of matter
Combustion

BACKGROUND

Whether they are on a birthday cake or dinner table or menorah, most candles we use today are wax-dipped candles. This style of candle dates back to the ancient Romans. Through the center of the wax runs a wick, which is usually made from cotton or other material that can absorb liquids well. So how do these two materials come together to help a candle burn steadily?

A lit candle might seem simple, but it is actually an example of a multi-step process resulting in combustion—and the glowing flame you see. Combustion is the result of a chemical reaction in which oxygen gas reacts with the substance that is being burned. The combustible material in a candle—or its fuel—is the wax. However, before the wax can become fuel, it first needs to get hot enough. To start that heating process, you need to light the wick with another source of fire, such as a match. As the wick burns down, the heat of the flame melts the wax around the wick. Because the wick is absorbent, it sucks the liquid wax into the wick and upward into the flame. Once the liquid wax gets hot enough, it then turns from a liquid into a gas. The hot gas then reacts with the oxygen from the air and is burned, creating the candle flame that we see. This means that the candle flame is actually created by the burning wax gas—or vapor—and not by the wick itself or the solid, or even liquid, wax.

After lighting a candle, it might flicker or sputter at first, but then it usually burns fairly steadily. As the heat of the wax vapor flame melts more of the solid wax, it creates more fuel for the flame to burn. The candle will only go out once it runs out of wax or oxygen—or gets blown out. After a candle goes out, you can actually see the wax vapor escaping as a stream of white smoke. If you hold a match into that smoke, the candle will catch fire again—without even touching the wick! Don't believe it? Then try this activity to see for yourself!

MATERIALS

- Adult helper
- Several small, narrow birthday candles
- Matches or a lighter
- Wet sand (or another non-flammable substance to hold your candles up—you could also use cake or a cupcake!)
- Dish or bowl for your wet sand or other candle-holding substance
- Fireproof work area
- Straw
- Bowl filled with water or a fire extinguisher

PREPARATION

- Take your materials to a fireproof work area.
- Make sure you have an adult helper assist you while doing this activity.
- Keep the bowl of water or the fire extinguisher close throughout the activity in case you need it.
- Prepare your wet sand or other non-flammable base material in the dish or bowl.
- Stand one candle up in your wet sand or other material, packing it around the candle base to make sure it is secure.

PROCEDURE

- With the help of an adult, light a match. Hold the flame close to the candle's wick, but don't touch the wick with the flame. *What do you observe? Does the candle light?*
- Next, touch the candle's wick with the flame of the match. Hold it there for about a second. *What happens when you touch the wick with the flame?* If the wick did not ignite, light it now.
- Watch the candle burn for a couple of seconds. *Can you describe the flame? How does it look?*
- Blow out the candle and watch what happens. *Do you see white smoke escaping from the wick?*
- Light the candle again, then light another match. While the match is still burning, blow out the candle. Immediately afterward, hold the flame of the match into the white smoke of the blown-out candle, close to the wick but without touching it. *What happens? Does the candle light again? Why or why not?*

- Blow out the burning candle. Now stand two candles next to each other in your wet sand (or other material) so that they are secure and will not fall over. They should almost touch each other. Light both candles with a match.
- While both candles are burning, point the end of a straw toward one of the flames. Blow through the straw to extinguish just one of the flames. The other candle should keep burning. *What happens after you extinguish one of the candles? Can you explain your observation?*
- Repeat this step several times. *Do you always get the same results? Can you tell from your observations which part of the candle is burning? Why?*

EXTRA

Place three or more candles next to each other. With a straw, blow out one of the candles, but keep the others burning. *What happens to the blown-out candle?* Then blow out two of the candles, but keep one burning. *Can you see the flame jumping from one candle to another?*

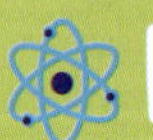

EXTRA

Try the activity with candles made of paraffin or beeswax. *Do you get the same results for these materials as well?*

EXTRA

Look at a candle's flame in more detail. *Can you see that the flame has different colors?* Do your own research to find out why there are different colors. *Can you find out which part of the flame is the hottest or coolest?*

OBSERVATIONS AND RESULTS

Could you make a candle's flame jump from one candle to another? The first time you lit your candle, you most likely had to touch the wick with the flame of your match. This makes the wick catch fire, which starts the combustion reaction. The wax around the wick starts melting, and it is from this liquid wax that vapor is created inside the flame. The wax vapor starts to burn and creates the stable candle flame that you see. When you blew out the candle, you should have seen white smoke rising up into the air from the wick. This is the wax vapor, which becomes visible as it condenses into small liquid droplets in the cooler air.

If you touched the wax vapor (white smoke) with another flame, the candle should have immediately lit up again. This time you didn't even have to touch the wick or another part of the candle. Lighting the vapor is enough to get the candle burning again. When you placed two or more candles next to each other and blew one out, the burning candle's flame should have reignited the wax vapor of the extinguished one. You might have realized that it is actually quite hard to keep a candle extinguished when it is so close to a burning one. It lights up again due to the fact that the wax vapor of the blown-out candle is touching the remaining candle flame. What you end up seeing is the candle flame jumping from one candle to another!

CLEANUP

Make sure to extinguish all your candles at the end of your experiment. Once the matches are cooled down, you can throw them in your regular trash. Clean up your work area and wash your hands with soap and water.

Make Elephant Toothpaste

SQUEEZE SOME SCIENCE: USE A LITTLE KITCHEN CHEMISTRY TO MAKE A FOUNTAIN OF "TOOTHPASTE" ALMOST BIG ENOUGH FOR AN ELEPHANT'S BRUSH!

Create a giant foaming reaction, and use science to wow your friends with this classic activity. With just a few ingredients, you can make something that looks like a foamy toothpaste being squeezed from a tube—but so big that it looks almost fit for an elephant!

PROJECT TIME

20–30 minutes

KEY CONCEPTS

Chemistry
Biology
Reaction
Catalyst
Surface tension

BACKGROUND

You might be familiar with hydrogen peroxide as an antiseptic used to clean cuts and scrapes, which it does by killing bacteria. But what is it? It is a liquid made from hydrogen atoms and oxygen atoms (its chemical formula is H_2O_2). It is available in different strengths, or concentrations. You usually find it in a 3 percent concentration. (Although higher concentrations are available, they are more dangerous and must be handled carefully.) It also breaks down when exposed to light, which is why it usually comes in dark brown bottles.

When hydrogen peroxide breaks down, it turns into oxygen (O_2) and water (H_2O). Normally this breakdown happens very slowly. However, you can make that reaction happen faster! How? By adding a catalyst. Yeast is an organism that contains a special chemical called catalase that can act as a catalyst to help break down hydrogen peroxide. Catalase is present in almost all living things that are exposed to oxygen, and it helps them break down naturally occurring hydrogen peroxide.

This means that if you mix yeast with hydrogen peroxide, the hydrogen peroxide will rapidly break down into water and oxygen gas. The oxygen gas forms bubbles. These bubbles would usually escape from the liquid and pop quickly. However, adding a little dish soap provides additional surface tension, allowing the bubbles to get trapped and creating lots of foam. This foam looks like a giant squeeze of toothpaste—almost big enough for an elephant!

MATERIALS

- Empty plastic bottle
- Dry yeast (found in the baking section of the grocery store)
- Warm water
- Liquid dish soap
- 3 percent hydrogen peroxide
- Measuring cups
- Measuring spoons
- Safety glasses
- Large tub or tray to catch the foam
- Location for the activity that can tolerate spills (of hydrogen peroxide as well as possibly food coloring), such as a kitchen or bathroom—or an outdoor location
- Liquid food coloring (optional)
- Different-shaped bottles or glasses (optional)

PREPARATION

- Put on your safety glasses to do this activity because hydrogen peroxide can irritate your eyes. (Note: Although the product of this activity resembles toothpaste, it is not toothpaste, so do not attempt to use it!)
- Gather your materials in the location where you plan to do your activity. Place your plastic bottle on the tray or tub so that it is easy to clean up all the foam.

PROCEDURE

- Measure 1/2 cup (118 ml) of hydrogen peroxide, and carefully pour it into the bottle.
- Add a big squirt of dish soap into the bottle, and swirl gently to mix.
- If you want to make your foam a single color, add a few drops of food coloring directly into the hydrogen peroxide, and swirl the bottle gently to mix. If you want to give your foam stripes like some toothpastes, put the drops along the inside rim of the bottle's mouth. Let them drip down the inside of the bottle, but do not mix.
- In a measuring cup, mix together 1 tablespoon of yeast and 3 tablespoons (44 ml) of warm water. Stir for about 30 seconds.
- Pour the yeast mixture into the bottle then quickly step back, and watch your reaction go! *What happens? How long does the reaction last?*

Try the activity without the dish soap. *What happens? How was the result different?*

EXTRA

Try the activity with different-shaped containers. *What happens if you use a bottle with a narrower or wider neck—or a cylindrical drinking glass with no neck?*

OBSERVATIONS AND RESULTS

You probably saw lots of bubbles and foam in this activity. What makes the foam appear? When the hydrogen peroxide comes into contact with the yeast, it starts breaking down into water and oxygen. Oxygen is a gas and therefore wants to escape the liquid. The dish soap that you added to your reaction, however, traps these gas bubbles, forming a foam. The reaction continues as long as there is some hydrogen peroxide and yeast left. Once one of them runs out, it stops making new foam. If you tried the activity without dish soap, the reaction probably still made bubbles—but not foam.

CLEANUP

Wash the foam down the sink when you are done with the activity.

Make Your Drawings Float!

DRAW AWAY! USE A LITTLE CHEMISTRY TO MAKE YOUR OWN MOVING SKETCHES.

Have you ever wished your drawings would come alive and the stick figures or objects on your paper could move around? It's not as impossible as it sounds! In this activity, you will make your drawing move around by letting it float on water. What makes this possible is the interesting chemistry of dry-erase markers. These markers are usually used to write on whiteboards or glass surfaces and can easily be erased. It turns out they are also perfect for doing science!

PROJECT TIME

20-30 minutes

KEY CONCEPTS

Chemistry
Polymer
Solvents
Materials science

BACKGROUND

You might have a whiteboard in your school classroom. To draw on this surface, your teacher probably uses a whiteboard pen or dry-erase marker. The writing from these markers can easily be erased from the whiteboard without leaving any marks.

This is possible because dry-erase markers contain special ingredients. They include a solvent, which is usually some kind of alcohol. This is used to dissolve the color pigments that determine the marker's color. In addition, a resin or polymer is added, which is the key to making the ink erasable. In a dry-erase marker, the resin is an oily silicone polymer, which acts as a "release agent." This makes the ink of the marker very slippery and prevents it from sticking to the whiteboard's surface. This is why the ink can easily be wiped off from a very smooth, nonporous surface such as a whiteboard or glass.

You might know dry-erase markers can permanently stain other surfaces, such as clothes. This is because fabric doesn't have a smooth surface, so the ink can soak into its pores—staining them forever! In real permanent markers, the resin used is an acrylic polymer that functions as a "binding agent" and makes the ink stick to the surface. Only the type of polymer differentiates a permanent marker from an erasable marker. Find out how this difference affects how your drawings float in this activity!

MATERIALS

- Two shallow trays or plates with smooth surfaces that you have permission to draw on with markers
- Dry-erase markers (different colors)
- Permanent marker
- Cup
- Water
- Rubbing alcohol
- Paper towels

PREPARATION

- Find a work area that can tolerate water spills.
- Fill your cup with room-temperature water and set it next to your trays or plates.

PROCEDURE

- Choose one color of your dry-erase markers and make a drawing on your first plate, such as a stick figure, a heart, or word. *Does it look like the ink is sticking to the surface of your plate?*
- Let it dry for a couple of seconds, and then use a dry finger to wipe across your drawing. *Does your finger wipe off the drawing, or can you still see it afterward?*
- If the drawing came off, make a new drawing. Otherwise, keep the old one. Then pour just enough water onto your plate to cover the drawing. Wait and observe. If nothing happens, shake the plate a little bit. *What happens to the ink after a while? Does your drawing begin to float and come to life?*
- Next, use a permanent marker to make a drawing on the second plate. *Do you see a difference from how the dry-erase marker looked on the surface?*
- Let it dry for a couple of seconds and use a dry finger to wipe across your drawing. *Does your drawing disappear once you wipe it with your finger? Can you explain why or why not?*
- If the drawing came off, make a new drawing. Otherwise, keep the old one. Then pour some water on your plate to cover the drawing. Wait and observe. *What happens to the drawing this time? Does it float? How are your results different from the previous ones?*

EXTRA

Make drawings with different colors of dry-erase marker. *Do all of them behave the same way or are they different? Which color floats best?*

SCIENCE FAIR IDEA

What happens if you pour rubbing alcohol on top of your drawing instead of water? Does your drawing still float? Do dry-erase and permanent markers give you the same result? Why or why not?

Can you erase your floating drawing? Try to pick up your drawing from the water's surface with your fingers. *What happens to it when you pull it out of the water? What do you think the material you now have in your hand is made of?*

OBSERVATIONS AND RESULTS

Did you get your drawings to float? You should have—but only when using the dry-erase marker. When you make your drawing on the surface of a smooth plate or tray, the solvent, or alcohol, that dissolves the ink ingredients will evaporate. This leaves the color pigment and polymer behind on the surface. With the permanent and dry-erase markers, it actually looks like the color is sticking. When you wipe across your drawing with your finger, however, only the drawing that you made with the dry-erase marker will disappear. This is because the oily silicone polymer in the dry-erase marker prevents it from sticking, whereas the acrylic polymer resin in the permanent marker makes it stick to the surface.

The fun starts when you pour water on your drawing. You should have observed that your dry-erase marker drawing magically detached from the plate and rose to the water's surface. There, it could float and move as if it were alive! The permanent marker drawing should have remained stuck to the plate. This difference is due to the special polymer in the dry-erase marker ink—because this ingredient prevents the ink from attaching to the plate, and the water can slip underneath. Also, because the ink is lighter than water, it can float. When you poured rubbing alcohol on your drawings, however, you should have seen them both slowly dissolve. This is because alcohol is used as the solvent in both markers.

CLEANUP

Remove all remaining drawings from your plates by rubbing them with a paper towel soaked in rubbing alcohol. Then rinse the plates with warm water and soap before reusing them.

Does It Sink or Float? Depends on the Soap!

NOW YOU SEE IT ... DRIP A DROP OF SOAP, AND FIND OUT HOW TO MAKE SURFACE TENSION'S POWERS VANISH!

If you've ever washed dishes, you know the right dish soap can make a dirty job a lot easier. Have you ever wondered how dish soap is able to clean dishes so much more effectively than water alone? Like many household cleaners, dish soap is a surfactant—it helps break up leftover food on plates by making it easier for food particles to dissolve in water. This soap also breaks up the water molecules themselves, which leads to some pretty interesting kitchen science! In this activity, you'll be observing some surprising properties of dish soap in water!

PROJECT TIME

10-15 minutes

KEY CONCEPTS

Chemistry
Surface tension
Surfactant
Molecules
Chemical bonds

BACKGROUND

Giant ships, people, and rubber ducks can all float on water's surface, thanks to one very important trait of water molecules: hydrogen bonds! Water molecules cling strongly to one another by forming these bonds from one molecule to another. They allow water molecules on the surface of water to behave like a membrane, which can even support the weight of small objects, such as water strider insects. This property of water is known as surface tension. You have probably observed this phenomenon many times in your life. Have you ever noticed a single drop of water sitting on your car windshield? Instead of flattening out or splashing, these raindrops are able to hold a spherical shape because the water molecules comprising the raindrop are more attracted to one another than they are to the windshield of your car. As a result, those molecules hold tightly to one another, forming the raindrop's spherical shape.

Surfactants such as dish soap break up water's surface tension. As a result, objects floating in water will sink or change shape as the surface tension changes. In this activity, you'll explore how surface tension affects the behavior of objects in water—and why it's so important!

MATERIALS

- A bowl
- Water, enough to fill the bowl at least halfway
- Liquid dish soap
- A rubber band
- A metal sewing pin

PREPARATION

- Fill your bowl at least halfway with water.

PROCEDURE

- Place your rubber band on a table or other flat surface. Notice its shape when it sits on the table.
- Place your rubber band into your bowl of water. Notice the shape of the rubber band when it is in the water. *Does it look different than it did when it was on the table? If so, what is different about it?*
- Place your pin in the water in the center of the rubber band. *Does the pin sink or float?*
- Drop a few drops of dishwashing liquid into the water surrounded by the rubber band. Notice the rubber band's shape. *Did anything about it change when you added the liquid soap?*
- Observe the pin. If it is still floating, add a few more drops of liquid dishwashing soap. *Does the pin continue to float or does it sink? Why do you think this is the case?*

OBSERVATIONS AND RESULTS

In this activity, you used dishwashing soap to examine how surface tension affects the behavior of objects floating in water.

In the beginning of the activity, you should have noticed that the rubber band and the pin floated on the water's surface. They float because water molecules hold on to one another in a way that creates surface tension. This property allows many things to float on water, including your rubber band and pin. You should also have noticed the rubber band had a loose, or irregular, shape. It did not hold a perfectly round circle but instead floated in a shape similar to what it looked like before you put it in the water.

When you added the dishwashing soap, however, you should have observed a change in the behavior of the rubber band and pin: The band should have suddenly popped out into a circle. In addition, you should have noticed that adding the dish soap caused the pin to sink to the bottom of the bowl instead of floating.

Both of these results happen for the same reason—and you probably already guessed it has something to do with dishwashing soap, which is a surfactant and designed to break down water's surface tension. This helps make it an excellent cleaner. After you added the dishwashing liquid to the center of the rubber band, the surface tension on the inside of the band broke down. The water on the outside of the band, however, hadn't come in contact with the dishwashing soap. As a result, the water on the outside of the band still had strong surface tension, which caused it to pull the rubber band outward in all directions. This made the rubber band pop suddenly into a circle shape.

Similarly, after you added the soap to the water, you should have seen the pin sink to the bottom of the bowl. Because the soap broke down the surface tension, the water could no longer support the weight of the pin.

CLEANUP

Pour the water down the drain and dry the bowl. Put away your other materials.

Mix It Up with Oil and Water

A LITTLE MIX-UP: USE KITCHEN CHEMISTRY TO MAKE OIL AND WATER BLEND.

You may have heard people say, "Those two mix like oil and water," when they're describing two people who don't get along. Maybe you've also noticed shiny oil floating on the surface of water puddles after it rains. In both cases, you understand that water and oil don't go well together—but have you ever wondered why? So many other things can dissolve in water—why not oil? In this activity, we'll explore what makes oil so special, and we'll try making the impossible happen: mixing oil and water!

PROJECT TIME

20–30 minutes

KEY CONCEPTS

Chemistry
Surfactants
Density
Polarity

BACKGROUND

Unlike many other substances, such as fruit juice, food dyes, or even sugar and salt, oils do not mix with water. The reason is related to the properties of oil and water. Water molecules are made up of one oxygen atom and two hydrogen atoms. In addition to having this very simple structure, water molecules are polar, which means there is an uneven distribution of charge across the water molecule. Water has a partial negative charge from its oxygen atom and partial positive charges on its hydrogen atoms. This polarity allows water molecules to form strong hydrogen bonds with each other, between the negatively charged oxygen atom on one water molecule and the positively charged hydrogen atoms of another. Other molecules, such as salts and sugars, are able to dissolve in water because of its polarity as well. The charges at either end of the water molecule help break up the chemical structures of other molecules.

Oils, by contrast, are nonpolar, and as a result, they're not attracted to the polarity of water molecules. In fact, oils are hydrophobic, or "water fearing." Instead of being attracted to water molecules, oil molecules are repelled by them. As a result, when you add oil to a cup of water, the two don't mix with each other. Because oil is less dense than water, it will always float on top of water, creating a surface layer of oil. You might have seen this on streets after a heavy rain—some water puddles will have a coating of oil floating on them.

In this activity, we will test the power of surfactants to help us mix oil and water. The surfactant we will use is dish detergent, which helps break up the surface tension between oil and water because it is amphiphilic: partly polar and partly nonpolar. As a result, detergents can bind to both water and oil molecules. We'll see the results of this property in this activity!

MATERIALS

- 2 clear plastic water bottles with lids
- 2 cups (473 ml) of water
- 1/2 cup (118 ml) of oil (olive, cooking, or vegetable oils will all work)
- Liquid dishwashing soap
- Clock or timer
- Permanent marker
- Measuring cup
- Measuring spoon
- Food coloring (optional)

PREPARATION

- Remove any labels from your water bottles.
- Use your marker to label the bottles: Label the first "Oil+Water" and the second "Oil+Water+Soap." Write the labels as close to the tops of the bottles as possible.
- Pour 1 cup (236 ml) of water into each bottle.

PROCEDURE

- Carefully measure and pour 1/4 cup (59 ml) of oil into the bottle labeled Oil+Water. Allow the bottle to sit on a countertop or flat surface while you observe the water and oil. *Does the oil sink to the bottom of the bottle, sit on top of the water, or mix with it?*
- Repeat this step, adding 1/4 cup (59 ml) of oil to the bottle labeled Oil+Water+Soap. *Does the oil sink to the bottom, sit on top of the water or mix with it?*
- Carefully add 3 tablespoons (44 ml) of dish soap to the bottle labeled Oil+Water+Soap. Try not to shake the bottle as you add the dish soap.
- Make sure the bottle caps are screwed on tightly to each bottle.
- Holding a bottle in each hand, vigorously shake the bottles for 20 seconds.
- Set the bottles down on a flat surface with plenty of light.
- Note the time on your clock or set a timer for 10 minutes.

- Observe the contents of each bottle. Hold them up to a light one at time so you can clearly see what is happening inside the bottle. *Did anything change when you shook the bottles? Do the mixtures look the same in the both? If not, what is different between them? How would you explain the differences that you observe?*

- After 10 minutes have passed, look at the contents of the bottles and note the changes. *What does the oil and water look like in each bottle? Has the oil mixed with the water, sunk to the bottom, or risen to the top?*

Add food coloring to the water to get a lava lamp effect.

EXTRA

Test other types of soap, such as toothpaste, hand soap, and shampoo by mixing them with oil and water.

OBSERVATIONS AND RESULTS

In this activity, you combined oil and water, then observed how adding dish detergent changed the properties of this mixture. First, you should have noticed that when you added the oil to the water, they did not mix together. Instead, the oil created a layer on the surface of the water. This is because oil is less dense than water and therefore floats to the surface. When you shook the Oil+Water bottle, you might have noticed the oil broke up into tiny beads. These beads, however, did not mix with the water. After you let the Oil+Water bottle sit for 10 minutes, you should have observed the oil and water starting to separate again almost immediately, and after another 10 minutes, there were once again two distinct layers in your bottle.

In contrast, you should have found that shaking the Oil+Water+Soap bottle resulted in a lot of foam, but instead of immediately starting to separate, the mixture was a cloudy yellow color. Eventually the oil and water should have separated into two layers again, but these layers should have appeared less distinct and cloudier than the layers in your Oil+Water bottle.

The difference between the two bottles results from adding dish detergent to the Oil+Water+Soap bottle. The detergent molecules can form bonds with both water and oil molecules. Therefore, although the oil and water aren't technically mixing with each other, the dish detergent molecules are acting as a bridge between oil and water molecules. As a result, the oil and water molecules aren't clearly separated in the bottle. Instead, you see a cloudy mixture, resulting from the oil, soap, and water chains you've created by adding dish detergent.

CLEANUP

Dispose of your water and oil mixtures with an adult's help. Do not pour oil into the sink as it can clog the drain. Rinse and recycle the plastic bottles.

Charge from Change
Make a Coin Battery

ZIP-ZAP! MAKE A LOW-VOLTAGE BATTERY TO LIGHT UP AN LED—AND LEARN HOW CHEMISTRY HELPS POWER MANY OF YOUR PORTABLE ELECTRONICS.

Have you ever wondered exactly how your phone, laptop, or a flashlight manages to work without being plugged into a power outlet? Where does the electrical energy come from that makes all these portable devices function? You probably know the answer: They use batteries! However, do you know how these batteries work? Batteries store electrical energy in the form of chemical energy, which means that electrochemical reactions inside the batteries create electricity. It may sound complicated, but it is simpler than you think! In this activity, you will create a basic homemade battery with just construction paper, vinegar, salt, and a handful of pennies and washers—and prove it works by lighting an LED!

PROJECT TIME

30-40 minutes

KEY CONCEPTS

Chemistry
Electricity
Battery
Chemical reaction

BACKGROUND

Electricity is the presence of an electric charge, which can be either positive or negative. An electric current is generated by moving charges, usually in the form of electrons or ions. In batteries, these moving charges are created from chemical reactions, meaning electrical energy is derived from chemical energy. The main components of a battery are two electrodes, typically made from carbon or two different metals, and the electrolyte, which is a liquid or paste that is in contact with both electrodes. The electrodes and electrolyte need to be electrically conductive to allow electrons and ions to flow from one electrode to the other. The question now is: Where do the electrons come from? Here is where chemistry comes into play.

Electrons are generated via electrochemical redox (reduction-oxidation) reactions, in which negative charges (in the form of electrons) are transferred from one chemical (or metal) to the other. The electrons and ions released during these reactions travel through the electrolyte from one electrode to the other. During that process, one electrode releases electrons while the other accepts them to complete the electric circuit. There are many different battery types that use different chemical reactions to generate electrons; two common ones are lithium-ion and nickel-cadmium. In this activity, you will make a copper-zinc battery using a vinegar and salt solution as the electrolyte. Do you think your battery will generate enough electricity to power an LED?

MATERIALS

- 20 metal washers (galvanized; the size of a penny)
- 20 pennies (preferably shiny)
- Pencil
- Construction paper
- Scissors
- Bowl
- Vinegar
- Table salt
- Spoon
- Small white or red LED
- Paper towels
- Work area that can tolerate vinegar spills
- Calculator (optional)
- Aluminum foil (optional)
- Multimeter (optional)

PREPARATION

Note: In this activity, you will make a very low-voltage battery. The amount of electricity generated by this homemade battery is safe; higher voltages of electricity, however, can be very dangerous and even deadly, and you should never experiment with commercial batteries or wall outlets.

- Trace a coin 20 times on the construction paper with a pencil.
- Cut out all the coin-size paper pieces.
- Pour some vinegar into a bowl and add enough salt to create a saturated solution, which means not all of the salt is able to dissolve. Mix with a spoon.
- Put 15 of the coin-size paper pieces in the bowl and let them soak in the vinegar-salt solution for five minutes.

PROCEDURE

- Take one washer and place it on your work area. *What material is the washer made of?*
- Take a soaked construction paper piece and place it on top of the washer. *Why do you think the construction paper needs to be soaked in the vinegar-salt solution?*
- Next, place another washer on top of the soaked paper piece.
- Then place another washer on top of that washer. Add another piece of soaked construction paper and then add two more washers on top of that.
- Repeat alternating the soaked paper and two washers until you have used nine washers in total. You should finish with two washers on top of a soaked piece of paper.

- With a paper towel, dry off the sides of your washer stack. You want to make sure it is dry on the side.
- Also, check that the soaked paper is not touching more than one washer on each side.
- Take the LED and spread the two contact pins apart. Then push the long pin of the LED underneath the stack so that it makes firm contact with the washer on the bottom. Place the short pin on top of the washer on the stack and press it down. Watch the LED. *Does the light turn on when you connect the pins to the top and bottom of the washer pile?*
- Make a second stack in the same way, but this time use pennies instead of washers. *What material are the coins made of?*
- Once the penny stack is complete, dry it off on the sides and ensure the soaked paper only touches one penny on each side.
- Then, take the LED again and connect the long pin to the bottom coin and the short pin to the top one. *Do you see the LED light up when you make contact with the coins?*
- Make a third stack, but this time, start with a penny on the bottom, place a soaked paper piece on top of the coin, and then add a washer on top of the paper. Repeat, adding a coin, soaked paper, and washer, until you have used five coins in total. You should end up with a coin placed on top of a washer.
- Again, make sure to dry any excess liquid from the soaked paper on the side of the coin-washer stack, and check that the soaked paper only touches one washer and coin on each side.
- Then connect the long end of the LED pins to the coin at the bottom of the pile and the short end to the washer on top of the stack. *What happens to the LED this time?*

- Finally, use the dry construction paper pieces and make a fourth stack, alternating a coin, a dry paper piece, a washer, a coin, a dry paper piece, and a washer until you have used five coins. *Do you think it makes a difference if the construction paper is wet or dry?*
- Take the LED one more time and connect the long pin to the bottom of the stack and the short pin to the top. *Does the LED light up this time? Why or why not?*

SCIENCE FAIR IDEA

How many coins and washers do you need to light up the LED? Does the amount matter at all? Try lowering the number of coins and washers you stack. *What is the minimum number of coins and washers you need to light up the LED?*

SCIENCE FAIR IDEA

What would happen if you exchanged the washers with another type of material, such as aluminum foil? Would you still get a functional battery? Cut coin-size pieces of foil and create a stack of coins and aluminum to find out!

EXTRA

If you have a multimeter at home, you can measure the voltage of your battery and how much current it produces. *How does the voltage and current change as you add more coins to your battery?*

OBSERVATIONS AND RESULTS

Did you manage to get the LED to light up? Probably not with the first two stacks, which consisted of only coins or washers. Pennies are coated with copper, which turns your penny into a copper electrode for this activity. The galvanized washers, on the other hand, are coated with zinc, which is a different metal and functions as a zinc electrode in your battery. The key to a functional battery is that an electrochemical reaction has to occur between the two electrodes. If both electrodes are made of the same material, no reaction will take place and no electricity will be generated.

When you alternate the pennies with the washers, however, you create a battery with two different electrodes—one zinc and the other copper. Now an electrochemical reaction can happen between the zinc and copper that releases electrons to travel through the electrolyte (vinegar and salt-soaked construction paper) to generate an electric current. This is why the LED should have lit up in the third stack that you created by alternating coins and washers. When you removed the electrolyte and used dry paper pieces instead, the electrons were no longer able to move from one electrode to the other, so no electric current was produced and the LED did not light up!

CLEANUP

Rinse the coins and washers with tap water and dry them off. You can reuse them afterward. Discard the soaked construction paper and wipe down your work area.

No Stain, No Pain!

HOW TO SCRUB STAINS AWAY—
THE SCIENTIFIC WAY!

It's happened to most of us: You wear a brand-new shirt, and in the middle of lunch you get a giant ketchup stain right in the middle of it—or maybe it's peanut butter or spaghetti sauce. Whatever the stain, it's always ugly and can be tricky to remove. Did you know there are many different kinds of stains, and each requires different types of cleaning to get it out? If you try to clean a mustard stain using shower cleaner, for example, you probably won't get good results. Why does the type of stain matter? In this activity, we'll explore a few different kinds of stains—and try to determine the best method for cleaning them!

PROJECT TIME

30-45 minutes

KEY CONCEPTS

Chemistry
Acids
Absorption
Solubility

BACKGROUND

There are many different types of household cleaners because there are many different types of messes to clean up! Stains can be roughly grouped into four different categories: enzymatic (such as grass or blood stains); oxidizable (such as coffee or tea); greasy (such as butter or oil); and particulate (your typical, run-of-the-mill dirt stains).

Enzymatic stains are generally the result of protein action, and therefore enzyme cleaners will help break down these proteins into smaller, soluble (able to dissolve in water) chunks. Oxidizable stains are usually brightly colored, such as juice. These stains are removed by using a bleaching agent—for example, hydrogen peroxide. These oxidizing agents break down the color-causing components of chemical structures so that the stain becomes invisible! In the case of greasy stains, the best cleaners are usually surfactants. Surfactants surround the greasy stain and expose the water soluble sections of the stain-causing chemical structure, helping it to dissolve in water and wash away. Finally, particulate stains are usually cleaned with compounds called builders. These builders help remove positive metal ions such as those of calcium and magnesium, breaking down tough dirt stains and allowing them to be washed away.

In this activity, we will test the cleaning power of three different cleaning solutions made from household products. We will evaluate how well they clean three different types of stains. Keep track of your results, and maybe you'll be able to add some science to the laundry when you're finished!

MATERIALS

- Three small cups (three-ounce size works well)
- 1/8 cup (29 ml) of white vinegar
- 2 tablespoons of cornstarch
- 2 to 4 tablespoons (29 to 59 ml) of milk
- 1/8 cup (29 ml) of hydrogen peroxide
- Nongel toothpaste or cream of tartar
- Water
- Piece of light-colored fabric that can be stained, such as a cleaning rag (Make sure to ask for permission from an adult before choosing your fabric!)
- Black marker
- Ketchup
- Coffee or tea
- Teaspoon

- Paper
- Pencil or pen
- Timer or clock
- Access to a sink
- Dishwashing gloves
- Flat baking tray
- Adult helper (This activity uses household chemicals that, if handled incorrectly, could be dangerous. Have an adult help you!)

PREPARATION

- Label your cups as follows: Cup 1 "Vinegar," Cup 2 "Peroxide," Cup 3 "Cornstarch," Cup 4 "Water."
- Pour the vinegar into your vinegar cup.
- Pour the peroxide into your peroxide cup. Add 1/4 teaspoon of cream of tartar or a nongel toothpaste. Stir to combine.
- In the cornstarch cup, combine your cornstarch and milk and stir to form a paste.
- Place your fabric on a flat, dry space (such as a countertop). If the surface under the fabric is not stainproof, protect it with some newspaper or a flat pan.
- Use your marker to draw a row of four marks on the fabric. Make sure to leave at least 2 inches (5 cm) between each mark, and try to keep them all in a line. Next to each mark on the fabric, make another small stain using ketchup, keeping at least 2 inches (5 cm) between the ink and the ketchup. Gently dab a small amount of ketchup in a second row next to the first ink row. Create a third row using the coffee or tea, gently dropping a small amount of coffee next to each ketchup stain, again making sure to keep 2 inches (5 cm) between the ketchup and the coffee stains.

- Use your paper and pencil to create a table with four columns and five rows. In the first row, label the columns: "Cleaning Method;" "Ink;" "Ketchup;" "Coffee." In the first column, label the rows: "White Vinegar;" "Hydrogen Peroxide Mix;" "Cornstarch and Milk;" "Control." This table will help you record your observations during this activity.

PROCEDURE

- Start with your vinegar cup. Use your teaspoon to carefully drop 1 teaspoon (5 ml) of vinegar across one row of different stains, so that you add 1 teaspoon (5 ml) of vinegar to one ink, one ketchup, and one coffee stain. Set your vinegar cup down next to this row. *Did anything change when you added vinegar to the stains? Which stain is the darkest? Which is the lightest?*

- Start your timer for 10 minutes.

- Rinse your teaspoon with water, then use it again to carefully drop 1 teaspoon (5 ml) of peroxide (from your peroxide cup) across one row of different stains, adding 1 teaspoon (5 ml) of peroxide to an ink, a ketchup, and a coffee stain. Set your peroxide cup down next to this row.

- Repeat this step again, gently dropping your cornstarch paste onto one of each stain. (If the paste has hardened, add a small amount of milk and stir.) *What do you notice about the cornstarch and milk mixture? Is the consistency different than the other cleaning methods you're testing?*

- When your timer goes off, put on your dishwashing gloves and carefully carry your stained fabric to the sink.

- Rinse each stain for 10 seconds with cold water, including the row of untreated stains. Use your fingers to gently rub the fabric as your rinse the stain.

- Gently squeeze any remaining liquid out of the fabric, and place it on the baking tray.
- In your table, rank the ink stains from darkest to lightest. The most faded stain should be a 1 and the least faded stain should be a 4. Do the same for the ketchup and coffee stains.
- Look over your results and compare the cleaning solutions with the control stains. *Does any cleaning solution have all 1s? Does any cleaning solution have all 4s? Did a cleaning solution work well for one type of stain but not for others? Overall, which cleaning solution worked best? Which one worked the worst? Was one of the stains more difficult to remove than the others?*

EXTRA

Repeat this activity testing other household products and foods that commonly cause stains—for example, mustard or cooking oil. Compare your results.

EXTRA

Test whether leaving the cleaning solutions on the stain for a longer period of time changes your results.

OBSERVATIONS AND RESULTS

During this activity, you experimented with three different household products to see how effectively each removed different types of stains from fabric. Although all of these products are excellent stain removers, they each work in a different way and therefore are most effective with different types of stains.

To start, vinegar works as a very effective household cleaner because it is an acid. Acids remove stains and clean by adding a chemical charge to the stain's molecules. Much like a magnet being pulled by another magnet, these newly charged molecules become attracted to the positive and negative charges in water. As a result, they pull away from the fabric and can be rinsed away with water. Vinegar works well on dirt, mold, and mineral deposits as well as on other acid stains, including coffee. Therefore, you may have found vinegar did a good job removing your coffee or tea stain.

Hydrogen peroxide works differently than vinegar and is better at removing different types of stains. Hydrogen peroxide doesn't actually remove stains—it just makes them invisible! It breaks up strong chemical bonds in stains, including ink, and in doing so it makes the stains colorless—but they're still there! As a result, you might have found in your tests that peroxide did the best job of "removing" the ink stain.

Finally, cornstarch works well as a stain remover because it attracts and absorbs the molecules of the stain. Cornstarch works especially well on grease stains and food stains, so you might have found it did a good job with the ketchup stain on your fabric.

CLEANUP

Discard the fabric used in your experiment. Wipe down your work area. Wash your hands with soap and water. Put away the materials used.

Make Your Own Lava Lamp

WHO KNEW SCIENCE COULD BE SO FAR-OUT? WITH A LITTLE KITCHEN CHEMISTRY, YOU CAN MAKE YOUR OWN COOL LAVA LAMP!

Have you ever seen a lava lamp? They might look complicated, but you can make your own using common kitchen supplies. Try this activity to find out how!

PROJECT TIME

20-30 minutes

KEY CONCEPTS

Chemistry
Molecules
Buoyancy
Density
Polarity

BACKGROUND

If you look around your kitchen, there are probably a lot of different liquids, including water, juice, milk, and oil. Many of these liquids have different properties that you can see, feel, and taste. For example, milk is opaque and white, whereas water is transparent and clear, and oil has a "slimy" texture that makes it difficult to clean if you spill it.

Each liquid also has other properties that might not be so obvious because you can't "see" them easily. For example, they all have different densities (the amount of mass per unit of volume). Many common household liquids, such as juice and milk, have a density very close to that of water, so you might not notice a difference. Oil, however, has a lower density than water, meaning it can float on top of water. (It is buoyant.) You can see this if you try putting a few drops of oil in a glass of water—they will float on the surface.

Liquids are all made up of molecules that have different chemical properties. Some molecules are polar, meaning they have unbalanced electrical charges. These molecules tend to mix with one another better than they mix with nonpolar molecules, which have evenly distributed charges. You can observe this if you try mixing different liquids together. For example, it's very easy to mix together juice and milk or water and food coloring. However, if you try mixing water and oil—even if you stir vigorously—the liquids "want" to stay separated.

What can you do with all this information? In this project, you'll use it to make your own lava lamp!

MATERIALS

- Clear glass
- Tap water
- Vegetable or mineral oil
- Food coloring
- Alka-Seltzer tablets
- Flashlight (optional)

PREPARATION

- Prepare a work area where you can easily clean up any spills, such as a kitchen counter.

PROCEDURE

- Fill your glass about 1/4 full with water.
- Add several drops of food coloring.
- Fill the rest of the glass with oil (not all the way to the brim).
- Break an Alka-Seltzer tablet into four roughly equal-size pieces.
- Drop one of the pieces into the glass. *What happens?*
- Wait for the bubbles to stop, then drop in another piece. *How long do the bubbles last for each piece?*

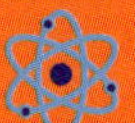

EXTRA

Stand a large flashlight on its end, with the light facing up, and place the glass on top. Turn off the lights in the room and turn the flashlight on. Drop in another Alka-Seltzer tablet, and you've made a lava lamp!

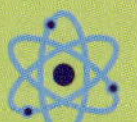

EXTRA

Try the activity with different temperatures of water. *How does water temperature affect your results?*

EXTRA

Try using half a tablet or even a whole tablet at once. *What happens?*

EXTRA

Try pouring some salt into your glass instead of using an Alka-Seltzer tablet. *What happens?*

EXTRA

Try reversing the order in which you add substances to the glass. *What happens if you pour the oil in first, then add the water and food coloring?*

Review the information in the Background section. Try making a lava lamp with different liquids you can find in your kitchen. *What combinations of liquids work, and which ones don't? Can you figure out why?*

OBSERVATIONS AND RESULTS

When you pour the oil into the glass, you should see it does not mix with the water—it forms a separate, clear layer on top. This occurs for two reasons: First, the oil and water are different densities—the oil is lighter, so it stays on top. Second, the water (and food coloring) molecules are polar, so they are strongly attracted to one another. The oil molecules are not polar, so they don't mix with the water or the food coloring. This is why you'll get the same result no matter what order you pour substances into the glass—the water and food coloring will always sink to the bottom instead of mixing with the oil.

When you drop an Alka-Seltzer tablet into the glass, it sinks to the bottom. It sinks straight through the oil without any chemical reactions occurring. When it touches the water, however, a chemical reaction occurs that releases carbon dioxide gas bubbles. These bubbles are less dense than the water or the oil, so they float to the top—but they "stick" to the water a bit, dragging some water droplets up toward the surface with them. When they reach the surface, the gas bubbles pop and the water droplets sink back to the bottom—creating a lava lamp effect.

Eventually the Alka-Seltzer tablet will be completely consumed, and the chemical reaction will stop. If you let the glass sit still, all the water droplets will sink back to the bottom. (Remember, they don't want to mix with the oil.) However, as long as you have more tablets, you can keep the reaction going!

CLEANUP

Do not pour all that oil down the drain! It could cause a serious clog. Ask an adult for help disposing of it. Options may include putting it in a sealed container in the trash or pouring it outside. If necessary, use towels to clean up any spilled water or oil.

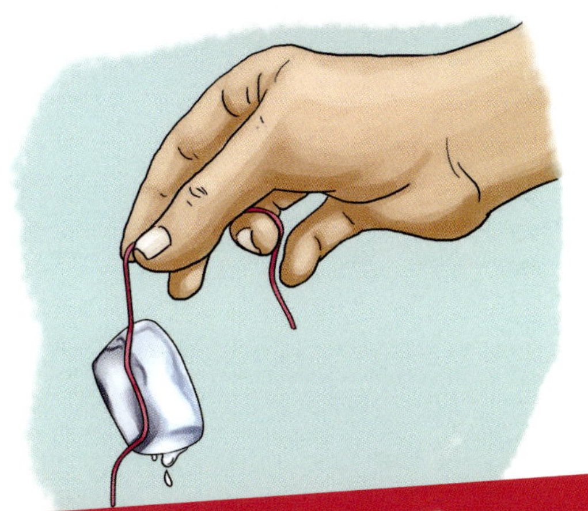

Lift Ice Cubes with Chemistry

MELT AND FREEZE YOUR WAY TO SOME SCIENCE MAGIC—ALL IT TAKES IS A DASH OF SALT!

Did you ever wonder why they use salt to de-ice roads? Did you know that snow more readily sticks to pavement treated with salt? Why would this be the case? In this activity, you will use the same principles to pick up ice cubes with a string. Is it possible to do this—without getting your hands cold? Do the activity and see what a pinch of salt can do!

PROJECT TIME

30 minutes

KEY CONCEPTS

Chemistry
Freezing
Melting
Freezing-point depression

BACKGROUND

Water is made up of tiny building blocks called molecules. These water molecules don't sit still—they wiggle and move around all the time. The water's temperature is a measure of how much these molecules move. When you cool water, you lower its temperature, and the molecules slow down. Eventually, after you cool the water enough, they move so little they can form strong connections, and the water freezes, turning into ice, which is a solid. For pure water, this transition happens around 32° Fahrenheit (0° Celcius). Conversely, if you add heat to a block of ice, its molecules will start wiggling more; eventually they move around too much to stay stuck together, and the ice melts, turning back into a liquid. These transitions, however, do not happen instantaneously—water and ice can coexist. (That is, a whole ice cube does not turn to liquid water all at once.) To visualize this process, you can think of a group of excited children—like molecules at higher temperature, they move and wiggle a lot. The higher their excitement, the more they move. Calm them and they will slow down just like molecules slow down when you reduce the temperature. Eventually you might get these children to hold hands and stand nicely in line—so they behave like a solid.

When the water is not pure, the water molecules cannot connect as readily to form a solid; other particles get in the way. That is why salty, sugary, or other water solutions' freezing points—temperatures at which they turn solid—are lower than 32°F (0° C). This explains why treating roads with salt in winter can prevent them from icing over. The salt dissolves in the water, lowering its freezing point, which will only turn to ice at temperatures well below 32°F (0° C). In this activity, you will use this characteristic in a clever way to pick up an ice cube.

MATERIALS

- Ice cubes
- Three glasses
- Cold water
- Salt
- Three strings, each about 8 inches (20 cm) long (Yarn works well.)
- One sticky note
- Watch or timer
- Thermometer (optional)

PREPARATION

- Gather all of your materials on a work surface that can tolerate spills.
- Fill your three glasses with cold water.

PROCEDURE

- Put a few ice cubes in the first glass of water. They float because ice is less dense than water.
- Search for a cube whose surface is at about water level. Lay one end of a piece of string across that ice cube. *Do you think the ice will stick to the string?*
- Lift the string. *Does the ice cube stick to the string? Why do you think this is the case?*
- *Do you have ideas on how you can lift the ice cube with a string, without touching the cube with your hands?*
- Try again, but now, sprinkle some salt over the string and ice cube. *Do you think the ice will stick to the string if you lift it?*
- Lift the string. *Does the ice cube stick to the string? After all, salt is not glue, right?*
- *What do you think would happen if you left the ice cubes with the strings on top out for a few minutes?*
- Take the two other glasses filled with water, and add a few fresh ice cubes to each glass.
- For both glasses, lay one end of a piece of string across an ice cube whose surface is about water level; let the other end of the string hang over the edge off the glass.

- Sprinkle salt over the string and ice cube in one of the glasses, and mark this glass with a sticky note. Wait for about two to three minutes. *Do you think the ice will stick to the string after you give it some time? Would both, only one, or none stick? Why would this happen?*
- After about two to three minutes, lift one string at a time. *Can it pick up the ice cube? Can you explain what you see?* If you cannot pick up any ice cube, try again but wait a little longer this time.

SCIENCE FAIR IDEA

Try some other substances, such as sugar or food coloring. *Can these make the ice cube stick to the string?*

SCIENCE FAIR IDEA

Make two identical water-and-ice baths. Add more salt to one bath; leave the other as is. Measure the temperature of each water-and-ice bath every minute for the next five minutes. Graph your results. *What do you observe? Is one colder than the other? Why would that be?*

EXTRA

Can you re-create a mini iceberg in a saltwater ocean in a bowl at home? What temperatures can prevent your "iceberg" from melting and "ocean" from freezing?

OBSERVATIONS AND RESULTS

Could you lift the ice cube you had sprinkled with salt and left untouched for few minutes? Did you fail to pick up the cube in all the other cases? Why does this happen? First, the ice around the string melts when you sprinkle it with salt, then the string freezes to the ice cube.

You probably wonder why it happens only when you sprinkle salt over the ice cube and string. When you sprinkle salt over ice, it dissolves in the thin layer of water above the ice. Because saltwater freezes at a lower temperature than pure water, adding the salt makes some ice melt and absorb heat in the process. The area just around it thereby cools and freezes water molecules to the ice cube, also freezing the string on. Without the salt, the water and ice are both at the same temperature and the string does not freeze to the ice. In both cases, the ice cube gradually melts as it absorbs heat from the air around it, but without the salt, the string cannot freeze to the cube.

If you used sugar, you would see the same effect. The cube sticks to the string. Dissolving other substances in water will also lower the freezing point and create the same effect.

CLEANUP

Pour the water and ice cubes in the sink, and wash the glasses.

Sudsy Science

Not All Shampoos Foam Alike

HAVE SOME GOOD, CLEAN SCIENCE FUN—AND LEARN HOW SHAMPOOS DO ALL THE DIRTY WORK—WITH SOME AT-HOME CHEMISTRY!

We lather our scalps with shampoo all the time. However, what exactly makes a good shampoo? You might be surprised to hear every new shampoo has to pass lots of scientific tests before it is considered good enough to be sold. Many different shampoo recipes are compared to decide which is best for the consumer. One of these tests assesses the foaming behavior of the shampoo. In this activity, you will become a cosmetic scientist and put different shampoos to the test. Which brand do you think creates the most foam and which foam lasts the longest?

PROJECT TIME

45 minutes

KEY CONCEPTS

Chemistry
Water
Oil
Surfactants
Foams

BACKGROUND

Although many different shampoo products are available in stores, they all have the same purpose: to clean dirt and greasy oil from your hair and scalp. How can shampoos remove all this built-up oil? For this, shampoos contain specific ingredients called surfactants, which are the main ingredients in shampoos besides water. Surfactants have a useful chemical structure that has a hydrophobic (water-repelling) tail and a hydrophilic (water-loving) head. This property allows them to react with both water and oil, which normally doesn't mix with water.

Although its cleaning power is probably the most important criterion for a good shampoo, there are many other aspects that decide the quality of a shampoo. Besides surfactants, there are also additives in each shampoo that optimize its look, feel, scent, or performance, such as additional foam builders, thickeners, conditioning agents, or preservatives. For example, the ability to create lots of foam and control its stability is important because people associate more foam with more cleaning power. Although this is not necessarily true, a shampoo sells better if it makes more foam. Therefore, additional surfactants that are able to produce extra foam are often used as foaming agents.

Scientists continue to research new shampoo recipes and have developed specific tests to assess each new product they create. This allows them to compare different shampoo recipes to find the one formula that performs best overall. In this activity, you will perform such a test yourself and find out which of the shampoos in your selection creates the best and the longest-lasting foam!

MATERIALS

- Selection of different shampoos (at least two different kinds)
- Disposable cups (8 ounces [236 ml], one per shampoo)
- Kitchen scale
- Tap water
- Spoon
- Measuring spoon (tablespoon)
- Tall, narrow glass, jar, or vase (larger than 8 ounces [236 ml]), preferably with lid
- Stopwatch
- Two permanent markers (two different colors)
- Tape
- Paper and pen
- Ruler
- A workspace that can tolerate spills

PREPARATION

- Use the permanent marker to label each cup with the name of the shampoo you want to test.
- Make a 10 percent solution of each of your shampoo samples. To do this, put one empty cup on a kitchen scale and zero it. Add 20 grams of your shampoo sample and then add tap water to the cup until the scale reads 200 grams.
- Carefully mix the shampoo with the water by stirring with the spoon.
- Repeat these steps for all of your shampoo samples. Clean your mixing spoon between each sample.

PROCEDURE

- Get your tall, narrow glass and carefully pour about 6 tablespoons (50 ml) of the first 10 percent shampoo solution inside. *When pouring the shampoo into the glass, do you already see any foam formation?*
- Have a timer ready and set it to five minutes.
- Put the lid on the glass if you have one. (If you do not have a lid, use the palm of your hand to cover the glass and seal off the top.) Then take the glass between your hands and shake it very hard 10 times up and down. Do your best to keep the shaking speed constant for all shampoos. *What happens once you start shaking the shampoo solution?*
- Immediately after you are done shaking, start your timer. Place a piece of tape to mark on the glass the level at which the foam phase starts (at the bottom, right above the liquid) and where it ends at the top. (You can use the marker to write on the tape to note which shampoo sample it is.) *How much foam did the shampoo produce?*

- To assess the foam's stability or to determine how fast it disappears, place pieces of tape to mark the foam levels (top and bottom) on the glass after five minutes. (You can use a different color marker to distinguish this measurement.) Note: The foam levels are likely to change most at the interface between the liquid and the foam, not at the top of the foam layer. *What happens to the foam over time? Do you have more or less foam after five minutes?*

- After you have marked the foam levels, clean out the glass (making sure all the shampoo and foam are removed) and look at the different marks you made. Take a ruler and measure the distance between the top and bottom levels of the foam layer at the beginning and after five minutes. Write your results down on your paper. *How did your foam volume change over time? What do your results tell you about how stable the shampoo is?*

- Remove the tape from your glass and repeat these steps for each of your shampoo samples. *How do your results compare? Which shampoo made the most foam? How much foam disappeared for each shampoo within five minutes? Can you correlate the foaming behavior with a specific shampoo ingredient?*

- Finally, repeat the steps with pure water. *Do your results differ when using just water compared with the shampoos? If yes, why do you think this is the case?*

Find out how long your foam lasts and increase the time you monitor the amount of foam in your glass. *At what time point is the foam completely gone?*

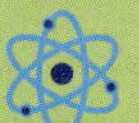

SCIENCE FAIR IDEA

Many natural shampoo brands reduce the amount of surfactants and additives in their shampoo recipe because these can potentially irritate the scalp. Compare a natural shampoo brand to a standard one to see if they make the same amount of foam.

SCIENCE FAIR IDEA

You can also make your own shampoo from recipes you find online. *How does your homemade shampoo compare with the store-bought product? Does it work well in cleaning your hair?*

OBSERVATIONS AND RESULTS

Did you create lots of foam? Most of the store-bought regular shampoo should have produced lots of foam once you started shaking it. You might have even seen a little foam formation already when you poured the shampoo solution into the glass. This is because these shampoos contain lots of surfactants and foam builders. When you shake the glass, you create lots of gas bubbles that get trapped in the shampoo solution and result in the foam you see. The surfactants or foaming agents facilitate the formation of foam and stabilize the gas bubbles in the solution.

The foam, however, is not stable forever! In fact, you should have observed the amount of foam quickly decrease over time, and probably saw the bottom level of the foam quickly rise to a higher level. This is because the gas bubbles in the solution eventually collapse. The volume of foam you produce for each of your shampoos depends on the amounts of surfactants and foaming agents they contain. Solutions that do not contain any of these substances, such as water, do not create any foam, which you should have noticed in your last test.

CLEANUP

Rinse out the glass, dispose of each of the cups you used, and clean your work area.

THE SCIENTIFIC METHOD

The scientific method helps scientists—and students—gather facts to prove whether an idea is true. Using this method, scientists come up with ideas and then test those ideas by observing facts and drawing conclusions. You can use the scientific method to develop and test your own ideas!

Question: What do you want to learn? What problem needs to be solved? Be as specific as possible.
Research: Learn more about your topic and refine your question.
Hypothesis: Form an educated guess about what you think will answer your question. This allows you to make a prediction you can test.
Experiment: Create a test to learn if your hypothesis is correct. Limit the number of variables, or elements of the experiment that could change.
Analysis: Record your observations about the progress and results of your experiment. Then analyze your data to understand what it means.
Conclusion: Review all your data. Did the results of the experiment match the prediction? If so, your hypothesis was correct. If not, your hypothesis may need to be changed.

GLOSSARY

absorbent: Able to take in and hold liquid.
bond: A force that holds atoms together in a molecule.
catalyst: Matter that causes a chemical reaction to happen.
condense: To change from a gas to a liquid.
dissolve: To mix with a liquid and become part of the liquid.
electron: A small part of an atom that has a negative charge and moves around the atom's nucleus.
extinguish: To cause to stop burning.
formula: The list of ingredients for doing something.
ignite: To begin burning.
ion: An atom or group of atoms that has a positive or negative charge because of gaining or losing electrons.
molecule: The smallest part of a substance that has all the properties of that substance.
opaque: Not letting light through.
phenomenon: Something that can be seen and studied and may be hard to understand or explain.
pigment: Matter that gives color to something.
polymer: A chemical compound that is made of small molecules arranged in a structure that repeats and forms a larger molecule.
portable: Able to be carried or moved around.
preservative: Matter added to something that keeps it in its original state longer.
solvent: A liquid used to dissolve a substance.
surfactant: A substance that is active on the surface of something.
transparent: See-through.

ADDITIONAL RESOURCES

Books

Debbink, Andrea. *Kitchen Chemistry*. Middleton, WI: American Girl Publishing, 2021.

Gray, Theodore. *Molecules: The Elements and the Architecture of Everything*. New York, NY: Black Dog & Leventhal Publishers, 2018.

Scholastic, Inc. *My First Science Experiments Book*. New York, NY: Scholastic, Inc., 2021.

Websites

Discovery Education
sciencefaircentral.com

Exploratorium
www.exploratorium.edu/search/science%20fair%20projects

Science Buddies
www.sciencebuddies.org/science-fair-projects/project-ideas/list

Science Fun
www.sciencefun.org/?s=science+fair

Videos

"Chemistry | Science Trek"
ny.pbslearningmedia.org/resource/idptv11.sci.phys.matter.d4kche/chemistry/. PBS Learning Media, 2:41.

"Fire Chemistry with the Cincinnati Fire Department"
ny.pbslearningmedia.org/resource/211-fire-chemistry-video/science-around-cincy/. PBS Learning Media, 5:56.

"What Is Chemistry?"
www.gpb.org/chemistry-matters/unit-1/what-is-chemistry. Georgia Public Broadcasting, 5:20.

INDEX